Wake

Relief to wake,
Justify the mistake,
Mistake of nothing,
Only boundaries,
Only love,
Only friends,
Only thoughts,
Only feelings,
Feelings peeling painfully
away the layers of scars,
Day after day,
Year after year,
Now i almost have no fear,
But the thought creeps in each year,

Yet the sun still rises,
And the sun still sets,
Let us not forget us my dear.

Brother

Brother,
Jolly fat and round,
Proud smug smile,
Genetically similar,
By blood we are bound,

Brother,
Outspoken and queerly funny,
Flying Angel wings,
Young king,
My sibling in all things,

Brother,
Childlike and full of pride,
Giggling at me,
Caring always,
In the distance you reside,

Brother,
Stubborn and scarred,
A broken heart,
Love thee,
I do; i am never far,

Brother,
Older and looking for home,
Searching searching,
Lost out there on your own,
Younger i am yet wiser
mayhaps i be,
You declared i was far more
intelligent than thee,
Marvelling at all i have
become,
Yet you have come,
Farther and farther than
anyone hath foreseen,

Be proud,
Young king,

Brother,
Isolated and alone,
Remember when you are sad,
You are never alone,
For i am your Sister,
And by blood we are bound,
We may at times be lost,
But we can always be found.

Saint Mary

Arisen,
Arisen into the dawn,
the dawn that welcomes a new day,
a new day for me,
for me to be shining bright,
bright like the sun,
warm rays of washing heat,
washing heat swelling with happy vibes,
happy vibes given over to by her,
by her who is flawless,
flawless and saintly,
Saint Mary,
Mary spreading love,
love with care and endearing loyalty,
loyalty that betroth her to my kin,
my kin and soul mate,
soul mate; sister and friend,
and friend who i give keys to,
keys to hearts of my blood,
my blood so beautiful,
beautiful with golden curls of silken hair,
silken hair with jade eyes of mine own sight,
sight full of innocence,
innocence that we both covet,
both covet with a mother's love,
a mother's love needs no explanation,
no explaination to justify why,
justify why this saint has the right,
the right as my chosen kin,
kin to bare my child like her own,
her own heart beating with care,
care for me,
for duty,
for life,
for all that she is and gives,
Mary,
Saint Mary,
Flawless and fair,
Beautiful; A friend without compare.

UCAS Plight

UCAS,
yer arse,
easy of access,
aye,
successful,
naw,
try again,
aye aweright,
sorry your application has
been denied,
fuck fuck fuck,
yer jokin?,
am chokin on desperate tight,
hav ye goan daft,
am better than aww these,
please please please,
where's ma chance eh!,
where's the diverse nature,
no even an interview,
yer system needs re-educatin,
cause av been participating,
everyhin and aww hings,
wurkin and strugglin,
but naw,
am no worth it right?,

UCAS,
yer arse,
easy of access,
aye,
but a want my application
money back,
a waste of cash,
the time of ma life.

Nightmare in the West

Yellow face,
rubbery ruse,
straw hair and uncertain
moves,
run,
run you must,
flee the state of the future,
for the future is dark and full
of terrors,

This balloon with it's squeeky
voice,
dangerously floating over the
airwaves,
through cables and ears,
trumpeting,
trump,
trump,

A nightmare,
living in the west,
Maybe Canada would be best,
for Pres,
instead of the circus,
turning minds to doom,
a revulsion in anything that
isn't pale or them,
them,
lord strikith down the petty,
the evil,
the wretched,

nope,
it's still happening,
making it great again,
how,

by kicking out the darker
shades,
please keep the Kardashians
by the way,
we don't need them anyways,

i say,
come ye back to the continent,
come ye who are good and
fair,
come ye now everyone,
come ye all of who would
escape the fear,
the nightmare,
the circus,
the trump,
the end,

Rip America,
Lets make Europe great again.

Red

Red; bright, bloody and loving,
Full of rage,
full of DNA,
full of passion,
full of red.

Red,
the rose that blooms,
the rose that wilts,
the rose that dies,
red petals on the ground,
drying black and crisp.

Red; the fury in my eyes,
the colour on my lips,
and between my thighs.

Red dripping everywhere,
everywhere,
and never halting.

Hungover

Dizzy haze,
the awakening phaze,
urgh my head,
that furry taste,
where the hell am i?,
least the couch was comfy
anyways,
oh an a quilt,
i'll just doze,
still in the days before clothes,

Bang! bang! bang!
chink, THAWck..BANG!
that'll be the door shut,
durty stop out,
a see she had hers,
but nope,
he just popped out,

Coffee hen,
oh yes please,
get your hole last night,
i teased,
naw hen no me,
with a glint and a sarcastic
smile,

My brains still floating in
rose,
pink liquid,
a tasty poison,
i'm glad i tapped out when i
did,
didn't hear their noising,

My mate looks like eve,
freshly thrown out of eden,
believing,
her innocence was infact
taken,
hungover,
one eye closed,

I laughed,
laughed,
drank my coffee,
got my clothes,
and left,
hungover,
the light outside turned up the
dial,
my brain protested,
opened the front door,
plopped on the couch,
there i rested,
hungover.

Washing Machine

Swirling,
Swishing,
Rolling and tumbling,
A washing machine mind.

Loud,
Louder than super spin,
Over and over again,
Soon to fall out,
Or take me to bed.

To work,
Work shall see me through,
Unplug the washing machine,
Forget,
The whurring wheeling
screeching,
Round and round,

My mind sound,
Or so I tell me.

People

People are like waves,
they come and go,
and they never stay,

People are like the tides,
rising to great heights,
receding back into the depths,

People are like fishes,
swimming endlessly on in
shoals,
winding fluttering swarms,

People are plural,
plurals like the seas,
connected and always moving,

People shape the earth,
like water shapes the rocks,
carving out a new space and
edges,

People are perception,
seeing is believing,
the seas are rising,
and the seas will swallow us
all.

Delicious is the Devil

Sexy,
Delicious is the devil,
The truth of your desire,
Feel the voice of silk,
The touch of pearls,
Take the hand,
Dance and make no deals,
Let it be merry,
Let it be wild,
Writhe and spill together in time,
Once upon a midnight dream,
Pick up all that you own,
Leave the devil wanting,
Sexy,
Delicious,
And wanting more.

Queen

Queen,
Be a queen,
And rule your own life.
Be loyal,
Be royal,
Wear your crown with pride,

Don't hide,
Shake it,
Leave all the haters waiting in line,
It's your time to shine,
Head held high,
No fucks given,

Wear that crown with pride,
Be royal,
Be loyal,
Rule your own life,
Be a Queen.

On the shore

What a pretty view,
Sitting here with you,
My head on your shoulder,
A few bottles between us,
The shore breathing in and out,
I could almost hear your heart beat,
The water against the rocks,
I glance at the blue and white,
Fluffy clouds sailing by,
Warmed by the sun,
It beams from the left of me,
A heart of gold.

Sitting with you,
On the shore.

Pretty

Pretty,
Pretty with lips of red,
Pretty in green,
Black skirts and wedge heels,
Pretty lost in the music,
Pretty smiling in a sensory bombardment,
Ardent for a good time,
Dancing under rainbow lights,
To the sound of days gone by,
Pretty walking tall,
Pretty knowing all; that this is a rare thing,
To feel pretty, beautiful and happy,
To dance and to sing,
Pretty having fun,
With lips of red,
And a crown of freshly cut gold upon her head.

Enter the Coliseum

As the crowd cheered,
As champions fought,
Sweat dripped from every pour,
As they poured out their pain,
As the lights danced in a frantic frenzy,
And the music roared the city to sleep,
Beckoning the eyes of the world,

Divas took their place,
As women and as true superstars,
Rick got flaired,
And a new belt was now theirs,
A pretty thing,

But then,

As the prince that would be king,
The prince that was promised,
Fell a many dizzying feet,
There unto his destiny,
Oxygen left the room,
The dead man walks again,

As the electricity intensifys,
The rock stood tall,
And the eaters men slane,

The banshee roared her proclamation,
All hail the king of kings,
You dirty sheep do follow,
Bow unto him,
The crowed stirred in motion,
Not unlike a swirling ocean,
To the thrall of his spectacle,
Here enter the roman,
The fight to begin,
As the crowds cheer and the crowds binge,
On goosebumps crawling up their arms,
Third time's a charm,
No matter who you are,

As the bell rung,
It didn't matter who won,
As seconds ticked by,
As the minuets caused more pain,
As time moved forward,
And their lungs faltered,
In the Coliseum of the immortals,
History…. was made.

Now gimmie a hell yea.

Poet

Poet,
What is a poet,
Do they know it?,
Do they show it?,
Do they rhyme all the time,
Do they free verse a lyrically diverse stanza?,
Is a poet romantic,
Or are they slamming,
Jammin out word and after word in absolutely powerful verse,
Spoken aloud,
To a crowd uncertain of the vocabulary highs they will endure next,
An emotional purge,
Does a poet know what they write,
rightly yes,
And writely no,
Woe is the heart of a writer,
So full of promise and wishful thinking,
Yet the poets heart is solar,
Its holier and full of scars,
But touched upon surrounded by shimmering stars,
Lighting the way forward through the blinding dark,
Hitting demons with the tap of a keyboard or scratch of a frantic pen,
Men hath feared worst things,
But the poet fears none and all,
The poet brings change,
The poet brings all,
A new perspective,
For one and all,

Do they show it?,
Do they know it?,
Poet.

Managers Message

Beep,
My phone weeps,
Ominously crying out a warning,
Something,
Something haunting,
A gripping stress,
Passive aggressive at best,
Or at least,
A feast of fear for my brain to alarmingly gorge upon,
The message is all about the return of one,
One that leads,
But instead bleeds a heavy burden all of its own,

I'm not ill anymore it speaks,
But I have alot of work for you this week,
I know you're off,
And so you shall be on,
No matter what plans you have,
Or where you have gone,
Heal to me,
Heal and know thy service is mandatory,
No rest for your wretched soul,
Work work work work work,
Scan this,
Move that,
Paper work do,
Oops I forgot to tell them that,

In this working world so small,
The manager returns to reign over them all,
Haunting,
My phone weeps,
Beep.

Ferry

Leaving the mainland,
Leaving for softer sands,
For waves,
And for the salty sea air,

Ferry me away,
Ferry me to peace,
Ferry me to breathe,
And to feel at ease,
Ferry me far across the sea,
To an island,
With a beach,
And lots of trees,

Walk with me,
Collect rocks and pretty shells,
Pretty things,
As the sea sings,
Sings her endless song,

Ferry me there,
Away to heavens cove,
Ferry me with you,
Stay till the dusk grows cold,

Ferry me back to the mainland,
To reality,
To a sort of hell,
To home.

(Ferry, is one of my favourite poems that I have ever written.)

No love like this.

No love like this,
Ever did write on a page,
Insane and unsociological,
It subverts the norm,
But my friend,
It is us,
And we it,

There is no love like this.

Mordern Survivor

Survive or die,
Norms thrown to the wild,
Without prejudice it lashed at them,
Depriving them of all nourishment,
Bear stood watching,
The experiment,
the reality,
To catch a fish,
To filter water,
To function without moderninity,

Dry mouths,
Broken bowls,
Faints and sliced arms,
The island had it charms,
Soon they were all humans together,
Building,
Fighting,
Celebrating embraces were the hunters alarms,
Of success,
And survival,

Yet bear stood watching,
As the experiment goes on,
The show continues,
And man finds a new way to make a profit.

Crushed

Crushed,
Under rocks,
Heavy weights of a heavy mind,
Be kind,
Let it be,
I'll get through it,
Its down to me,
To ride it out,
So let it be,
Just sit down next to me,
And listen.

Don't Sit Down.

If I could be so rude,
To say no then I would,
But they sit,
They ask and expect,
So that I cannot possibly reject,
Them,
Them who would sit next to me,
In the occupied seat where my bag lives,
Oh wenches,
And men,
Don't you see my bag there?
It's a sign without compare,
Go sit elsewhere,

I don't appreciate being hemmed in,
But its a busy train the woman said,
Who gives a shit,
Just don't sit next to me,
I want to breathe,
And not have to suffer your sneezing,
Weezing,
Coughing next to me,
My personal space is two seats wide,
You're currently in it with your big fat hide,
Save me jebus,
For I am not rude,
I just wanna sit myself,
Without prejudice,
And that's the truth.

Writing Life

Writing in colour,
Writing in black and in white,
Writing in rainbows,
Cause every little thing is gonna be alright,

Writing in blood,
Writing in tears,
Writing in fear,
Cause such is life,

Written for me,
Written for you,
Written for them,
And written in to,
History or Herstory,
Just to be fair,

Writing memories,
Writing goals,
Writing quirks,
Writing critiques,
Writing perks,
Writing all and never stopping,

Writing well,
Writing about heaven and hell,
Writing without self indulgence,

Writing of how good we should be,
Writing for free,
Cause it's not all about me,

Writing for glory,
Writing from the heart,
Writing in colour,
Writing in black and in white,
Writing in rainbows,
Cause every little thing is gonna be alright.

Behind us.

Silently he works in the distance,
He talks to me with no words,
He only wishes me well,
Untill I fell or fall prey,
He shall step forward and lunge to my rescue,
But dare he trifle me so,

He shall go,
Race and panic,
And claim my heart to be his,
Its no true mystery,
But its all just history,

The past is behind us.

Home

Home,

Home is a safe place to be,
Warm,
Sheltered and secure,
A bed to lay my tired body,
Feeling safe to sleep,

But what if your house doesn't feel like home,
Because you're alone,
With empty rooms and things,
Things that do not love,
That do not comfort,
That do no sway any emotion,
You just wander it aimlessly going through the motions,

What if your home isn't a place,
It's a person,

For me there's no other,
To love,
To trust,
To care for,

To be with in life,
To rest my sleepy head beside,

Only him,
And him alone makes me feel like I'm at home.

Broke

Broke,

Broke by work again,
Broke cause I stayed from dawn till dusk,
Broke cause its all a joke,
I won't stay for long,

Broke,
Cause money is fleeting,
Bleeding,
Hemoraging,
Just to live,
Just to be at ease,
From the stress and endless worries,

Broke,
From pain,
Live, give and gain,
From rules and laws,
Labels and tables of charts unending,
Mark this,
And resubmit that,

Broke,
Cause it's all forced,

Cause your behind today,
And further back tomorrow,
The writings on the wall,

Broke because life's a bitch,
Broken and breaking,
Cracking and faking,
Take take taking,
Making all the world tick by,
Currency and time,
An imaginary friend or foe,

Woe,
Oh, here we go,
No one knows,

Broke.

Strange Reflections

Yesterday was strange,
Enlightened by history repeating,
How i used to be,
How i kept defeating,
The verbal kicking's,
And the endless beatings,
By those all so ignorantly unkind,

An evaluation,
A reflection of what was,
Of where i had been,
How far i have come,

From darkness i rose,
Burnt from ashes i grew feathers,
Wings of colour and light,
My heart a shield from which to defend,
And my pen a sword to offensively fight,
Combating the hate,
The mistrust,
The unjust,
Now i stand on the edge of life,
Wings spread,
An angel for love,

Life is too short to decay away,
to hide how one feels,
to shy away,
or give up,

So now, I declare my love,
And urge you all,
Be kind,
Understand,
Get out and do it all,
Reach for your dreams,
Be the human that beams,
brighter than them all,

Yesterday was strange,
But i am loved after all.

Overcome.

Completed,
Not defeated,
By the time or the deadline,
Achieved a feet of destiny,
Soon the mile will be apon me,
Going by fast as i overcome me,

At this age,
A top grade would be a miracle,
A wonderful thrill to wave around,
Parade and be smug about,
Believing everything will work out,
As it's supposed to,

Close to,
And closer still to the higher up education mill,
Determined,
Strong of will,
I am more than i was

yesterday,
Tomorrow i will be stronger still,

If you've achieved against the odds,
Give yourself a round of applause,
And be at peace,
Happy and still.

Haunt The Night

They haunt the night,
A movie so lucid,
Irrational prophecy,
Or patchwork memories,
Wrenching from depth of consciousness,
From warmth and comfort,
From one universe to the next,
joyful laughing with eyes shut,
Or crying blindly in the darkness,

They initiate the deepest of emotions,
Swallowing you whole and dragging you under,
Thunders, cloud and rain,
Witnessing something irrational,
Too far it has gone,
Like a thunderclap of lighting,
Sparks fly uniting awareness with reasoning,
Suddenly you can see,

A dark room,
A bed,
Maybe pictures or a TV,
With a sigh of relief,
Mumbled,
It was only a dream,
It was only a dream.

King Of Skulls

Upon the Castle sits,
A king of skulls,
There he waits,
Seeking only justice,
All of his own laws,
The cause is clear,
Because he does not fear,
Or so it would appear,
Yet his heart is in a good place,
Saving children,
Helping women,
No matter of race,
Yet the war goes on,
Endlessly,
He cannot stop,
He cannot die,
Lets be Frank,
Up is down and black is white,
There is no grey,

The Punisher am i.

Waiting To Pay

Bills to pay,
Cue's in which to wait,
Even on a telephone line,
Please be patient,
The disembodied voice announced,
Half hour later my phone credits run out,

Back and forth they throw me,
All just to pay my bill,
They drain more from me,
Exchanging number 1 hits,
For my ever growing rage,
Answer the dam phone i say!,

Sweet Adele singing lullaby's to me,
Through miles of signals and cables,
Her sweet voice cannot soothe,
The truth,
Of which I'm almost done,
Waiting to pay this wretched bill,

I wish they would stop,
Instil-ing,
Fear of nothing,
Just pay your gawd dam bill,
Your blood, sweat and tears,
Give it to us all,

Well i would,
If you'd just answer the phone.

True Feels

It's a niggly pinching feeling,
I think of them,
Of him,
How I yern to sit next to them,
But it is all just feeling,
Hard to say,
Hard to not say on a repetitive loop,
But,
I miss them,
All the time.

Knit Together

Knit,
And click,
Purl,
And twirl,
Knit together,
Knit apart,
The back,
And the front,
Knit with speed,
And purl with devotion,
Knit and click,
Sliiiiide it across,
Knit with attention,
Purl with affection,
Bind it off slowly,
And neat-ly,
Let it ly before you,
Admire it,
Feel it,
All the work you put in,
Weave the ends like a couple

tangled in thin bed sheets,
Forget not to bind with a knot,
With a kiss just to finish it all off,
Completion is yours.

Comforting Passages

Even when its all done,
You've been fired,
Impaled on impending reality,
It sinks in slowly,
A panic in quicksand,
Cause you took the wrong step,
Now utterly regret,
But never forget it was a journey worth having,
You cry a torrent,
Downloading tears,
Uploading new thoughts of miserable acceptance,
Clutching hard to the best bits,
Holding onto the personal space,
Hyper aware of how empty the house is,
Alone,
Alone,
Alone,
Sitting here in a fabric throne,
A bed of fleece and acrylic cotton sheets,
Stained by salty stars,
And fears now fading,
Trading them for love messages,
Comforting passages,
Of how we both feel,
Shit and been through the wheel,
Spinning,
Spinning,
Spinning,
Dizzy and disorientated,
But we hold each other firm,
And thusly conform,
Through fires thick and thin,
Love grows within,
Tomorrow is a new day,
Now sleep well,
Love you and let it begin.

Fired

Marred,
Tarred,
Barred,
Fired,
Your service is no longer required,

Dismissed.

These Beats

These beats,
These feets of creative melody,
Base to base,

Sound covering your face,
Emotions in a volumised ocean,
Physically convulsing and swaying in motion,
Ears deafened by its glorious purpose,
Brain dwelling in a feverous endorphin explosion,
A bliss,
Lyrics like kisses and blows,
Whose knows,
Music is another gateway to the human soul.

Turn it up.

Words to be Seen.

They'll never see these words,
And the words will never gaze back,
Crossing wires,
Wifi,
And paths,
These words i write,
These words I recite,
Downloaded from the hidden spaces in my mind,
For all to connect with,
But a few shall seldom see,
In a world drowning in itself,
Lavishly so,
How I am to know,
That you'll ever see these words,
And that the words will gaze back,
Their sight with wider eyes,
Discovering,
That the words are just black and white, Its the meaning and doing what's right,
Fighting for life,
Staying strong,
And hoping that all along,
Someone's reading this right,
What I write,
And what they wrote too,
Somewhere there's a writer out here just like you.

Scroll Addiction

All in phones,
Lost in zones,
Attached and addicted quietly,
Rightly knowing,
They should throw them away,
Alas in rows they stand silently,

Scroll,
Scroll,
Scroll,
To only scroll some more,
'Why am I looking at this?',
Its because you're addicted to pretty lights,
Petty Facebook fights,
And pointless news stories a plenty,

But we need these things,
Its become our way,
I'd rather have a book,
But society says; one must stay connected,

Infected by constant struggle and addiction,

This affliction will only grow more so,
Poor souls,
Sucked away into nothing,
By a glass screen?,
Have you seen yourself lately?

Maybe, put the phone down and look at the world,
It doesn't have a ringtone,
But lately it's a beautiful place to be.

Never Dissolving

Home is where the heart is.

My heart is in many places, my heart is love for many faces but my love is only true for one who blessed me with many graces,
who knows me more but doesn't say it,
who holds me close but keeps a distance.

My heart has been parted in many ways but this love has always remained the same, constant and evolving. More than words, here my heart and love remains unchanged never dissolving.

Bitter Sweet Victory

Good news,
It was just another stab,
Achieving shouldn't feel like this,
Hurtling down deeper into the dark,
Where demons claw,
Where your mind sees all the bad,
But it isn't bad,
Just hollow,
A hollow victory,
Bitter sweet like revenge,
Revenge that's realises its an asshole all along,
Disappointed,
Faded to liquid crystals rolling down the cheeks of a cliff,
Falling and consoling yourself,
That you did the right thing,
Life's not saying it hates you,
Just that it wants to wound you a bit more,
Another scar to condition and to wear as if it were armour,
But that glamour is for everyone else,
Deep down you feel sad,
Angry,
And wondering where to go now,

You got your medal,
Proud shining badge of "I did this",
But it lead nowhere,
Only to depression,
Yet do not let your demons destroy you just now,
Tomorrow is a new day,
Stay alive to find out,
Why we must cry our eyes out,
To get to see a cleaner clearer picture,

And the picture is still developing.

A Man's Time and Space

Peace,
Peace was all he wanted,
For the toil and the strain had taxed him,
Stress had rendered him a darker shade of blue,
Social pressures put apon him unrealistic,
He just wanted to stick to the couch,
All alone,
And not move.

They weighed in from every direction,
Come give me attention,
Even when he mentioned,
That he wasn't in the mood,
Food for thought it was,
When he lashed out at them,
Again and again,
Yet they didnt listen,

How can a broken man be fixed in a day,
He thought aloud,
I just want time and space,
To think about my own feelings,
The good that lights my heart,
And the darkness that blankets the light with fear,
To be quiet and still,
Lost in my own world,
Just being pressured is enough to make me reel,
Reel backwards into myself,

He wanted to be alone,
At home,
With nobody but himself,
Im sorry, but it can't be helped.

Journey's Done.

It is done,
The long study,
The fearful epilogue to the journey now gone,
I am confident in my skills,
Lyrically thrilling,
Bone chilling,
Filling and zipping through your heart to the next dimension of provocation,
What location you ask,

Any you wish,
The next step is a massive leap of faith,
Hold on tight,
The ride is frought with drops so sheer,
It makes a cliff seem like a small mound of dirt and rock,
Tik tok,
Make your mind up,
Carry on trying,
Carry on crying,
And let it be known you tried hard,
Battle and prattle on proudly,

Life's dying to have you.

Have you not been taught?

Tit for tat,
This for that,
Selfish and youthful,
I want,
I want,
I want,
Have you not been taught,
What is good and what is not?

Selfless,
I don't want,
I don't want to talk like war,
A battle that can't be fought,
And won,
For one,
And not for all,

Put yourself aside to show them all,
It's for the soul,
For wholesome freedom to wish for someone else,
Luck and joy,
That this isn't a toy,
value what you have,
Not what you haven't got,

I thought for them before myself,
No matter what I really want,
I just want to help,

But my voice shall remain beneath all the booming static that drowns vital voices out.

Pen and Paper Love

Type and type,
Write to write,
But I love the way paper feels,
The pen in my hand,
Like companion I have always had,
Listening to my thoughts,
Things to be heard,
Things that should not,

My sweet long term lover,
How you caress my tears,
Elevate my fears,
Cherish my love,
Committing for eternity,
Sweet pages that may never be turned,

You're with me forever,
Till we both return to dirt,

My sweet pen,
My precious paper,
My heart owes you a debt,
A debt I could never repay,

One day my dearest friend,
The world will know thee well,
But we'll always be under each other spell,
We know each other all too well.

But I Forgive

I know i didn't quite get there,
One day maybe I'll be there,
But I forgive,
Myself,
For I did all that I could do,
I forgive you,
You did all that I needed you too,
I've been too hard,
On us,
On me,
But we will touch the stars together,
We shall see our sun rise,
Before our beautiful eyes,
My mind will be dazzled,
My soul a little frazzled,
But I'll see this through,
I'll get where I need to go,
And I'll always be right there for you.

Of Snow and War

Snow,
A bloody clash,
A shower of arrows,
Raining with fearsome folly,
Plunging down into the angry wolf,
His brother the ghost rode to meet,
In a game played by pups,
Sweet summer children,
Died so brutally,

A wave of men came rushing forward,
Wild and soldierly,
Brandishing steel sharper than words could ever cut,
Deep,
A wall of death piled on high,
Cut,
Strike,
Slash,
And trampled underfoot,
As horses raced through the mosh pit of war,

Bodies piled high,
One on the other,
A fortress of men,
A tomb for ghosts,
Suffocating and pregnant,
He saw the light,
Struggled up the fleshy pile to rebirth,

Amidst blood and smoke,
To breathe its foul smell,
Its life giving lung for filling prophecy,

The dogs of war barked,
Snapping in a line,
Dying all around,
Prayers answered as the mockingbird flys,
And with him he brings the win,

One dog was left,
And the wolf bitch said to his pets,
Eat and let it be done,
Let you be gone.
Bastard.

Sweet Ash

Blacker than ash,
With a dash of sweetness,
It's deeper than a well,
Silent and beautiful,
Grasp the cup it dwells in,
Over filling the sides,
Thus you can not tip it,
This way or that,
Just sip,
Just taste it's morning glory,
Like a nympho itching to be relieved,
As your eyes come unstuck,
And you casually say,
Holy fuck,
This is really good coffee.

Headlights

They look at me,
A deer in headlights,
Like they've never seen someone like me before,

They beam those headlights before me,
You there,
You know what you want to do in life,
Which is quite rare and unsettling,

Betting on me to win,
Or,
Betting me to fail,
Who cares?

It's my life,
I'll move it like a jet plane,
Or,
A wee rowing boat,

As long as I fly,
Or,
Float,
All will glide and sway with the tide,

Come heavens,
Or,
Ocean depths,
I will never regret,
Knowing what I want to do with my life.

Neither should you.

Depressed

There is no way i could possibly describe my feelings to you all,
For even i do not understand,
How could I be in such a state,
All because of failed plans,
I try not to write too self indulgently,
yet today i find myself worriedly off,

OFF? you say…

Yes … OFF…..

..off my food,
And off my life,
It's makes no sense,

All i ever wanted was to make a menze,
Once my life with a big fat nothing,
I don't want it to be that way again,

I am but a pretty face,
Chasing life and people,
Chasing a chance to know more,
To hold the door,
To swing it open,

But it's firmly rusted shut,
Just a small slither to grasp onto,
Frantically trying to pry it open,
It won't budge,

None of them will,
Like a blockage in my brain,
I'm trying to go past it,
Around it,
Over,
But it stares back at me with every turn,

I am hurt,
I am worse,
Depressed and thus it all stings,
even when i sing,
I'm crying,

I shouldn't be,
All i ever wanted for me,
Was to be happy,

But i guess happiness comes,
And happiness goes,
That WE should all feel some amount of sorrows,

Crying myself a river,
I only wonder,
What hell my mind will create next,

Depression is both,
Life and death,
Having a conversation in your mind,
Stabbing at your soul,
Goading you into irrational

thought,
Trying to soothe you,

Worried,
This self indulgence has gone too far,
But i must suffer it,
from sun rise till the night is finally dark.

BREXIT: A Chaotic Divorce

I dared not touch this,
But like an unwanted kiss,
I must address it,

Brexit,
A folly for over confident fools,
The height of ignorance,
Lies,
Lies and political spin,
Three hundred and fifty million was the winning number,
What a blunder,

Blind mice and sheep
Pointing fingers at more exotic creatures than their own,
Get out get out!!,
They shout with venomous spit,
If you're not white then you're not allowed In,
This fine English country, ha-ha leave win!!

Yet this United kingdom,
Britannia who ruled the world,
Is crumbling and splitting at its borders,
Only England and Wales voted out,

Out! ,
Out ! OUT ! OUT!!!

Here Scotland roar,
Naw ya bunch eh bams,
Our Niccy has a back up plan,
All are welcome to live,
To stay,
You are appreciated in everyway,
And we will wurk wae london too,
Because they seen sense to want to stay in the EU,

North of ireland may rejoin its former self,
A quick vote will help,
But Wales will always be England's coat tales,
Or back yard toilet,
But the dragons will know doom soon,

Soon,
This divorce will take place,
We'll just have to face,
And watch the borders rise,
New passports circulate,
The actual historical end of the uk,

These are dark days,
But in many ways for all of us,
In the west to the east,
I sincerely plead,
We find our humanity in peace.

Blair and The East

I remember,
Fire blooming on the tv,
Beasts growling in the night,
Buildings crumbling,
Dark words reporting,
And Blair announcing the near future,

I remember the death,
The protests,
All the speculations and questionable interest,
Reasons or the unfathomable consequence,

A heavy weight,
In a wall of death and terror,
The choice was made,
There forever the burden was his to carry,
A burden? Or a criminal act?,
A job? Or a leader?,

It didn't touch our shores,
Yet it knocked on the doors of soldiers,
Of their families,
Beckoning a revolt of trust,

But we must remember,
Looking to the east,
All that was lost,
In favour of eventual possible speculative peace,

Whatever comes,
let us be one,
Let us see no devide,
Let us find a way,

At the end of the day,
There is no place for that man to hide away,
From us,
His guilt,
Or death to say "its time."

Civil Heart

Sad,
When they leave my sight,
Never regret,
Hold on,
But don't fight,
Let it all be civil within your heart,
Know that they will never part,
From,
You,
You is the person they love,
A thing they covet justly,
Must they,
Be so far away all the time,
Away in other places,

In other spaces,
With different faces,

Yes,
For it was chosen,
Fated,
Do not see your heart frozen,
But a world of hope,
A warm spring still hot enough to dip your toes in,

To,
My frayed soul,
Its been many lifetimes,
let this be no different,
But a blessing in the end.

Fleeting

Fleeting,
Time streaming by from dawn till dusk,
Must,
I ask you,
Go home so soon?
For I only,
Wish for another,
Hour or two,
To be within our peace,
for me the days are weeks,
And the weeks are months,
And the months are years,
Gone to time,
Fleeting by so silently,
Apart from me you are alone,
My home,
So far away from me,
From us,
I must,
Make a point to plea,
Stay with me,
For I do not say goodbye easily,
As your heart touches mine,
When your bold arms wrap around me,
When will i see you,
I hope its not too long,
But your kisses are electric,
I want to stay in them,
Even long after you have gone,
Fleeting is the moments we love the most,
Even when your staring at the window,
Imagining the ghosts in your mind happy and full of smiles,
All the while,
The moment is fleeting past,
Belonging to history at last,
A few hours with you felt like a few minutes,

I admit it,
I am lost in the clouds,
Lost searching,
Yerning for home,
For you,
Always.

But I Deserve.

But i deserve to be,
More than am I now,

But I deserve respect,
More than I have had,

But I deserve to succeed,
More than my mind thinks I'm capable of,

But I deserve love,
More connected than in the distance,

But I deserve happiness,
More than i have ever had,

But I deserve stability,
More financial, more familiar, more balance,

But I deserve inner peace,
More than life has given me or the perception of my ever ongoing fate,

However life still has me in chains,
Waving the keys to freedom,
Like ghosts floating on the breeze,
In front of my face,
I can reach out but they only slip through my grasp like water,

Hotter than the sun,
My heart burns with sadness,
Only can this end with tears and sorrow,

But there's always tomorrow,
Maybe I won't feel so hollow.

Always and Beyond

A hundred miles feels like light-years,
The space between is an abyss I wish to conquer,
The time is fleeting by so fast
And yet,
So slowly I feel like a time lord lost in the hands of a pocket watch,
The silence is deafening and your voice mute,
Except from the moments flashing in my mind,
Ringing me to shaking on the inside like an addict missing a fix,

Yet this,
This is no true addiction,
No fiction,
No fantasy,
Nor twisted reality,

Just me,
Missing you,
All day long,
All night,
All morning,
All week long,

Even the occasional months
that have gone by without
you,

Without you things feel
wrong,
I don't feel at home,

But when you return,
I will tell you,
Express,
And fondly digress,
About how I have loved you
all along,

Then,
Now,
Always and beyond.

Flinched

I flinched,
I flinched from him,
As he went to kiss my cheek,
Through a barrier of fallen
hair,

I flinched from him,
As he tried to hold me closer,

Oh for I could feel his love,
His embrace wanting to be
warm,
Warm against my cold wall I
built around me,
I dare not wince,
I dare not let him in,

Nor see the pain that claws at
me,
He held me like he was sorry,
Like he loved me truly,
And yet foolishly denied
himself something sweet,

I flinched because I had to
fight to not let,
The tears stream down my
cheeks,

The man I love,
Loves me,
Loves me but no more,
No more than that,

As a matter of fact,
He's just a friend,
And that is that.

Sweet Child

Hold tight child,
Your sweet tears,
Hold the love in your heart and never forget it's wonderful warmth,
Oh sweet child,
You've tried so hard,
You've held your head up with grace,
But hid away in the dark,
Sweet child why do you cry?,
Why do you sigh and weep so quietly,
All alone,
Sweet child you don't deserve this,
To hate yourself so much,
Unclutch that rag from your fingers,
Come here and hold on tight,
I can't stay forever but I can stay tonight,
All you want is love,
Selfless love,
Someone to embrace you,
To understand,
To take your hand from time to time,
Sweet child can you feel my sorrow for you?,
All alone in there hiding,
Locked away in that tower of a mind,
Sweet child this is not your life,
This isnt your fate,
You are not the one you should hate,
You shouldn't hate at all,
But sweet child I understand it all,
I know of the thralls of the heart,
Unconditional love that has gone amuck,
A mess,
A shame,
A shambles and how it could drive someone insane with the slightest thought of betrayal,
Or,
Simple choice of a different path,
Love has free will,
And we have no control,
Sweet child, don't cry,
Hold me,
Hold me closer than ever before,
Let your heartbreak no more,

Love what you have and not what you have lost,
Love what you have become even if you cannot see the clearest picture,

Sweet child,
Look at me and see yourself,
See the woman you become,
Know that together we are one,
A beautiful sweet girl,
And an dutiful mum,
A child,
And her womanly self,

Sweet child, we don't have to go through this hell alone.

Death and Crying

She died,
I cried,
Each song and then,
He pried and poked,
But I wouldn't let him in,
Sad tears,
No fears,
Just numb and dripping in sorrow,
Forward to tomorrow,
Forward to life,

She died,
I cried,
And I cry still some more,
I'll accept once I close the door,
Maybe ill become a hero,
Maybe I'll paint the stars,
Maybe I'll let him try heal my scars,
But,
For now,
I cry softly on the inside.

Grieving Noel

Grieving,

Grieving is hard to explain,
To express what pain your are feeling,
Peeling away layers of memories,
Layers of moments,
Layers of time,
Layers of spaces shared,
All that was cared for and more.

Grieving,
How do you explain,
To a friend who has pushed you away,
But loves you still,
The chill as they try to comfort and be,
There,
It's not fair,
But I cant bare the stare of him any longer,
I flinch,
I wince and,
I wish I didn't feel this way any longer,
Angry,
But grieving,

Grieving is remembering the person lost,
But not forgotten,
Grieving is about writing them notes,
Birthday messages,

Buying flowers and leaving them places,
Or spaces they had been before,

What if it was to be,
That they weren't a hop, skip and a jump away from your door,
When a plane is vital,
And money is the key to its door,
Yet you don't possess any,
Not anymore,
Because you have nothing now,
No job,
Which you lost,
No university,
Which they dropped you from,
No purpose,
All the time,
Why can't I reach,
Or someone take pity on my life,
All I want right now is to fly,

Grieving,
Is an ugly mess of snot and tears,
Of navigating your worst fears,
Its loss,
Its pain,
Its damage to the brain,
Its hiding in bed,
It's pretending that they aren't dead,
Its wearing black,
Its singing in the back kitchen,
It's blue,
It's final,
Its death,

And death,
Death takes you in his arms,
I pray that she,
Is sleeping,
Peacefully,

Beautiful Noel,

A sun is gone,
But the stars have you,
My American dolly,
I will always miss you.

But right now i am grieving.

Little Fly

You're a buzzy fly,
Whizzing around like a little spy,
Lost in enemy territory,
Side to side,
You sit and watch,
Tasting sweet leftovers,
Investigating everything you see,
Getting closer to sneak a lim on my leg or shoulder,
But I swat you away with definity,
Because you little fly,
Are just but a pin head in my life,
I opened the window,
But you still remain,
Oh little fly I feel your pain,
But I don't want to relive it,

Now fly, you are bugging me,
Trying to steal a wanton sip from my coffee,
I'll wipe you left,
With a big fat nope,
This is no joke,
Little fly,
Buzz on back home.

Wherever that is.

The Lost And Found

Tried to shout,
Try to be loud,
But am I just another lost and found,
Relegated to the back of a dusty office,
Before someone takes a fancy,
And dances away with my romances,
Or lady purse filled with thing that are long forgotten in my mind,
Like tinder,
Burning with desire and hopeful zeel,
But five minutes later,
You hit delete or uninstall,
Cause the feels are real,
Flirting with thin air,
Oh! The humanity!,

Fuck it,
Just for profanity,

But like my purse,
With all its things,
Its false claimant does with it as they do with all things,
Throw it in the corner,
Forget it's there,
Forget it's beauty,
Without compare,
Depreciate and consummate its demise,
In a pile of other junk,
That's lower in your eyes,

But your blind vision,
Can't see the dimension,
Put me back please,

I am better in the lost and
found than with thee.

Anger

A rush of blood,
A well of hate,
I bathe in the flood of tears,
Cover my ears and hope it fades,
But,
Days after days,
The anger comes my way,
Wanting for it to be gone,
But its not fun,
When your hurt and irrational,

I wanted this thing,
This life so badly,
That failing has become maddening,
That trailing in line,
On eggshells,
On thin ice,
And false ideals,
Has led my wheels to spin and break,
Has caused myself pain,
All i wish is for it to go away,

Haven't I suffered enough?,
Of broken hearts,
Of unrequited love,
Of death,
Of tragedy,
Of false friends,
Of rejection by the convoy of truck loads,
Haven't I done myself enough pain as well?,
Shouldn't I be done,
Let go and let it all be well,
In the past,
Cause I have been a pain in the ass,
Or,
At least it feels that way,

Am I an awkward inconvenience,
Or a person to pity,
Do I fit with you still,
Or is it all just been sitting in a heart shaped box,
For later,
When you're ready?

Anger colours me blue,
It rages me green,
It covers me in black,
And wraps me in a quilt of solitude,
As if I myself am the problem,

No one can stop them,
Hurt is inevitable,
Whether to self or others,
The pain and guilt covers,
Like a choking noose of cling film,
I try to rake it off but,
I fail in that too,

Anger is always pain,
I don't want this,
I don't like what it says,

But even good takes a turn,
We crash,
We burn,

And so it is,
That we must learn,
To move forward,
Let go,
With or without closure,
And in turn heal our lives
once again,

But don't pretend it's all just
them,
The argument of empathy for
both the self and them,
Never ends,

Who are you?
What do you choose?

What kind of person will you
become,
Or,
Simply choose to let in,

Anger will always stretch us
thin.

Taxi Driver

I was feeling lazy,
Brazen because my bank was
refilled,
So I picked up a coffee,
Very jolly,

I strolled down the hill,
To the taxi rank,

I popped myself into the car,
To be greeted by the charm,
Of a taxi driver long past,
Gone far,
Believing in greater things,

Dips and swings,
His story broadly,
Started of with normal things,
Of school and college,
Of work,
Of nursing,
Of packing it in,
Cause he saw the light,
Or the light saw him,

He floated,
Touting his mystical wears,
I wasn't really prepared,
But I kept curious,
Interested in their,
Spiritual story,
Of being leeched from,
By spirits long gone,
Floating outside his body,

He wrote his story,
In poem,
And short,
He showed me,
I read it aloud then retort,
Change this word here,
Make it flow,
keep your catharsis so,

I don't think your mad,
Even so,
Taxi driver here's your fare,
I've got to go.

Hair Cut Smile

Wet,
The scissors chop away the
dead,
The split,
The ends,

Snip snip,
Brush,
Comb and clip,
With each I feel a little more,
Relaxed,

Cleanse,
Reshape and make it new,
Anything to feel better,

The chair holds me,
My head tilting in all
directions,
I look straight at my
reflection,
Watching a smile,
Grow upon my fair face,

In this,
I find peace,
Ease,
To be me,

It's just hair,
Scissors and straightners,
But it's feel good,

A positive move,
A change,

Watch me walk away,
With this smile on my face.

The Days

Oh the days pass,
They pass like a slow train,
Counting all the cars as they rattle on by,
Creaking to the tune of metal,
Clanking in the most specific way,
They drag like a speech gone on to long,
Or a song that seemingly knows no end,

Can I defend,
Or give my apology,
No,

They sit till like shadows,
Wordless,
Affectionless shadows,
Haunting me into isolated thought,

Self taught to not expect,
A message,
A call,
Nothing at all,
But hope is there none the less,

The days are silent creatures,
Ticking by at snails pace,

With grace and with beauty,
In this space,
I've come to recognise,
This life has become ugly,
And out of place,

The days stroll by regardless.

Close the DAM Door

Think of all the things you've made,
from day break to day end,
Think of all the achievement there's been,
Have you seen yourself,
For who you've truly been,
Why i ask,
Do you weigh on yourself,
So harsh,
Critical of those small mistakes,
Like blotches on your A grade paper,
Or that painting you said you'd fix later,
Why have you come to see,
yourself,
in such a pity,
A gritty tide lashing coarsely against your skin,
you bathe to wash it away,
But it stains like salt in an open wound,
Why let yourself be that way,
Negatively hounding yourself everyday,
When you could be making,
All of this go away,
You,
Yourself,
Everyday,
Do you understand this is no way to live,
To live is to laugh,
To love,
To enjoy all that you can,
Instead you sit there on your hands,
Believing there's nothing you can do,
To change,
To rearrange the life that has gone so south,
A cold exchange of waiting for the next day,
For pay,
For some miracle to come your way,
Just STOP!,
Think only a little,
Stop being so brittle,
And fall into love with yourself,
Maybe not just yet today,
But tomorrow,
This world is a harsh land,
With beautiful coastal edges,
Come sit on the edge of the world,
Admire all that you see,
Feel yourself feel,
Be as you want to be,
Don't come weeping into arms of those who won't have thee,
For they don't love just as you do,
They have minds and lives they live without you,
You can do the same,
There's no shame in being alone,
No shame in picking up a phone,
No guilt to shackle to you to

one place,
IF the signs are on the wall,
Your guts telling you to read,
Intake it all,
Then do so,
Bend and stretch,
Ease the tension in your neck,
In your veins,
In the cracks,
In your muscles,
In your mind,
Love and accept all that has come,
And gone,
Because it's done,
A haunting symphony it will be,
No more,
It's OK to close that door,
Let go,
Let yourself know,
That all hope isn't dead,
That you are sane and sad,
That all this WILL pass,
And that you can be truly positive once more,

Stop being helpless,
Just close the damn door.

Live Outside

This dark corner,
Stop living in it,
it's not your friend,
Just a check out point,
In your mind,
Stop,
Just get outside,
Make it there,
In the sunlight,
Walk,
And keep walking,

Don't think,
Just walk,
Keeping walking,
Looking all around,
Spot the things that are beautiful,
That are ugly,

Get outside of yourself,
And save thee.

Fever

Fever,
In the cabin,
Fever,
In the cabin,
Fever,
Fever,
Pressure,
Fever on my mind,
Cabin in the fever,
Fever in the mind,
Cabin pressure tighter,
Tighter,
Fever,
Cabins closing in,
By design,
Fever in the cabin,
Fever on the mind,
Fever breathing,
Feverish time,

Cabin fever,
Playing on the mind.

Fever.

Author Mystery

How do I put it on the page,
Let my story go,
There out in the world,
To be at the mercy of glancing eyes,
How do I pry my work from myself,
To throw it out into the world like a graduate throws their cap up in the air,
As if by chance someone would mistakenly catch it and take it home to live it's life without you,
How do you unburden such a story,
That has equally carried you from darkness as it has made you walk into it, to stare at its face,
To look upon yourself in a such a way it shows you truth,
How you see yourself,
How you see the world,

How do you print sunrises,
Or sunsets,
Standing on beaches with the one you love,
Drinking anything,
The smiles on faces,
Awkward things and awkward chances,
Passion,
Rejection,
Trees blowing in the wind,
Rain,

How do give the story the right ending?

Trust,
Trust me.

FIVE a.m Cat

Five A.M,
FIVE A.M AGAIN!,
Little silly floof can't you am sleeping?,
While you pity paw your claw into my cheek,
Pin pricking skin,
Defeating my will to sleep,
Or even just sleep in,
One or maybe two hours more,
I say,
As I toss you half caring to the floor,

You land on your feet with a mew,
But in a few- you'll be back,
To paw at me a new,
What was it you wanted anyways,
I'm awake now,
Yet you've scampered away,

Worse than a child,
You are,
So I slip back into bed,
My head on the pillow,
Sleeping almost dead,

Not five bloody minutes later,
A weight of fur,
Purrs and your sneeky little butt,
Has found a way to make a scarf,
Around my neck,
Fluffy suffocator,
Bugger off,
I'll pet you later,

I remove you once more to the floor,
You mew like a child wailing mum,
A prolonged drone of protest,
Till you find a way once more,
To pounce and wriggle,
And move like a stick insect,
Closer to my sleeping self once more,

Pay attention!,
PAY ATTENTION!,
MUuuuUM,
COME ON!!
LOOK AT ME,
I'm cute and floofy,

Stoopid little cat,
I catch a glimpse of those eyes,

And that look,
Yet that is that,

Im awake now,
Cause of you,
My stoopid little fluffy cat.

Printed in Poland
by Amazon Fulfillment
Poland Sp. z o.o., Wrocław